Brand Positioning Formula

The practical step-by-step guide to use Brand Positioning in your marketing

Marco De Veglia

*Plus an exclusive interview with
Jack Trout*

Brand Positioning Formula

The practical step-by-step guide to use Brand Positioning in your marketing

Copyright © 2018 by Marco De Veglia. All Rights Reserved.

Visit www.brandpositioningformula.com

The editorial arrangement, analysis, and professional commentary are subject to this copyright notice. No portion of this book may be copied, retransmitted, reposted, duplicated, or otherwise used without the express written approval of the author, except by reviewers who may quote brief excerpts in connection with a review.

United States laws and regulations are public domain and not subject to copyright. Any unauthorized copying, reproduction, translation, or distribution of any part of this material without permission by the author is prohibited and against the law.

Disclaimer and Terms of Use: No information contained in this book should be considered as financial, tax, or legal advice. Your reliance upon information and content obtained by you at or through this publication is solely at your own risk.

The author assume no liability or responsibility for damage or injury to you, other persons, or property arising from any use of any product, information, idea, or instruction contained in the content or services provided to you through this book. Reliance upon information contained in this material is solely at the reader's own risk.

Printed in the United States of America

First Printing: Sep 2018

ISBN-13: 978-1726475426

ISBN-10: 1726475425

"Brand Positioning is just how you differentiate your product or your company in the customer's mind.

Advertising is effective when it makes clear the Differentiating Idea of your Brand and gives a reason to buy."

Jack Trout

Contents

The Brand Positioning "missing manual"	1
What is Brand Positioning?	2
Does Brand Positioning work for small business?	3
Why you can listen to me about Brand Positioning	5
Why I wrote this book	6
Do you want to know more?	7
Brand Positioning Formula	8
STEP 1 Define the context	9
STEP 2 Find the Differentiating Idea	13
STEP 3 Test the Differentiating Idea	26
STEP 4 Brand Positioning Statement	30
Now you are Indiana Jones...	42
BONUS CHAPTER Final words from Jack Trout	44
Interview with Jack Trout, February 2017	45
How to go further with Brand Positioning	55
The author	57

The Brand Positioning "missing manual"

This book would have never been written without another book: Positioning by Jack Trout and Al Ries.

Actually, the whole modern marketing would have never existed without that book.

Philip Kotler, "the father of marketing" said:

"There is a step that shall precede the 4P of Marketing. This step is another P for Positioning, the revolutionary concept introduced by Ries and Trout in their book that has become a classic, Positioning."

Positioning – or Brand Positioning as I like to call it to link it to the Brand (more on that later) – has become the most used (and cited) "marketing concept".

And rightly so, because it is the most effective "mental model" to explain how marketing works.

And an evergreen model, effective in today internet and social media marketing world, as it was back in the late Sixties, when it was conceived.

What is Brand Positioning?

If you don't know the answer to the above question, I recommend you read the book that started it all, *Positioning*.

It is an enlightening read that will make you a better marketer and a better and "empowered" entrepreneur.

In fact, I wrote this book as the perfect companion to *Positioning*.

But, for your convenience, here is the answer:

Brand Positioning is putting your Brand in the customers' mind in a way that is different from competitors' and more interesting for your target.

If you have read *Positioning* you probably have been fascinated by this "mental model" that explains how marketing works and the inner working of the mind that you want to influence.

However, you probably have also found a problem.

No practical indication about how to use positioning in your business.

In fact, you can't find any "operating manual" that teaches you how to use Brand Positioning in your marketing.

And why there are not on the market manuals on how to use Brand Positioning?

I think the reason is the combination of two factors.

The first factor is that Brand Positioning has been invented and used for large companies and used by specialists (advertising agencies, corporate identity companies, large consulting companies) along with internal specialists (VP Marketing, VP Communications, Brand Managers), all supported by large resources.

There has never been the need for anyone to "learn" because there were people and resources with know-how.

This is totally different from the situation of the small business where the entrepreneur is directly involved in marketing, both strategically and practically.

For the entrepreneur it is key to learn *practical Brand Positioning*.

The second factor that *requires* a "practical manual on Brand Positioning" is that, once you understand the theory of Brand Positioning, how to apply it can be very subjective and leading to mistakes.

In my experience I have seen how the same Brand Positioning concept can be expressed in different ways (most not effective) because of this subjectivity.

In fact I have seen that some Brand Positioning ideas seem good, but have very little applicability, others are effective, others are irrelevant.

So, what about a practical manual for Brand Positioning?

But first, let's answer a question that maybe you have in mind...

Does Brand Positioning work for small business?

I don't know if you have – or, as a marketing professional or advertising agency, help – a small business or a big business.

But since there are more small businesses than big businesses I think it's worth to address this question:

Brand Positioning Formula

Does Brand Positioning work for small business?

Since its creation, Brand Positioning has been used for the marketing of big business. The reason is simple: it requires advertising (and PR), so it requires money, millions of dollars.

But today, with online advertising available for a few dollars to any business, everything changed.

Even small and very small business can use Brand Positioning.

And clearly, it works for small business.

I have the proof with hundreds of small business clients that I have helped teaching and consulting, to apply positioning to their companies with success.

In fact, while what I teach in this book works for businesses of any size, I wrote the book with small business in mind.

And, let me tell you this: I truly believe Brand Positioning is more important for the small business than for the big business.

Why?

Because small business can't waste marketing money: they have to find and communicate the right message.

And Brand Positioning does exactly that: help you find the right message and how to tell it.

Because, write this down: if you don't use Brand Positioning in your marketing, you are wasting money.

No social media, no funnel, no fancy creativity, no marketing investment works without an effective Brand Positioning.

And not only it is more important for small business: it also works better.

Again, why?

Because, still very few small business know and use Brand Positioning: it's a new thing in the small business market.

So it's fair to think your competitors don't have a clue. And when you hit them with your marketing driven by Brand Positioning it's like using a tank against enemies with bows and arrows.

Not fair. But you better want to be the guy in the tank.

Why you can listen to me about Brand Positioning

The final question you probably have is:

Why should you listen to you about Brand Positioning?

Good question: some info about your author are in order.

I have been working with Brand Positioning for about 30 years, starting in 1990 in an advertising agency, in Milan. Today I live in the US and consult with clients all over the world on Brand Positioning.

Working with agencies I did a special job called "Strategic Planner" who is the guy (or department) in ad agencies that devise strategies that drive creativity.

So I was a professional in applying Brand Positioning (the very basis of any marketing and communication strategy).

Brand Positioning Formula

After my years in agencies, I started to consult and focused on Brand Positioning and later also in its application in internet marketing and to small business.

I created the first online course on Brand Positioning and wrote the first Italian book on the subject.

In fact, in the course of my 30 years of work on Brand Positioning, I created a formula that I called **Brand Positioning Formula**.

This is the formula you will learn in this book and could apply to create your own Brand Positioning. Or your client's.

At the end of the day, the proof is in the pudding: read this book and try to apply what you will learn and see how it works.

I know that it works, because the Brand Positioning Formula is the exact formula I use to help my clients almost on a daily basis.

Why I wrote this book

I wrote a longer and more complete book on positioning and an online course, but there is a problem: they haven't been translated in English (yet).

Recently I was asked to write a report on Brand Positioning for a client in the US and thought: *why not make it a book?*

A book with just my Brand Positioning Formula, *a Brand Positioning manual* you can use for your business or your client business.

You won't find theory here: this is what I do with my clients every day to help them with Brand Positioning.

I didn't want to make it a long book, you should be done in a few hours of reading. The application will take what it will take, depending on your market and ability.

I also added a bonus chapter with my interview with Jack Trout. It's an exclusive interview, his last one.

In this interview, I asked him what he thought about some principles that I put in the Brand Positioning Formula. So what you will learn in this book has been "approved" by Jack Trout, the father of positioning.

I think you will *Brand Positioning Formula*. More important, I think it will be useful for your or your clients' business.

Brand Positioning works. And this is your Brand Positioning manual.

Do you want to know more?

I would love to be in touch with you. If you want to contact me and you like to learn more you can go to this site:

www.brandpositioningformula.com

Here you will find info and tools to make your Brand Positioning easier and more effective. And you could contact me and get support.

You can also contact me via email writing to

mdv@brandpositioningformula.com

Let's do Brand Positioning!

Brand Positioning Formula

In this course you will learn the 4 steps of Brand Positioning Formula, the system I have created to put Brand Positioning in practice.

This formula is comes from almost 30 years of Brand Positioning practice in several markets with business of every size and competitive stand.

In the first years as a Brand Positioning consultant, I based my work on the classic Positioning concepts I had learned in Ries & Trout books.

With time and practice, I understood that some things worked well and other were theoretical or at least very hard to apply in real life.

I have worked with big companies, but the most challenging and rewarding work with Brand Positioning I have done with small and very small businesses.

Here are the Brand Positioning Formula steps:

- Step 1: Define the context
- Step 2: Find the Differentiating Idea
- Step 3: Test the Differentiating Idea
- Step 4: Brand Positioning Statement

STEP 1
Define the context

The first, key concept to understand, is this: you have to be "competitor oriented".

Marketing is a battle of your ideas and perceptions against the ideas and perceptions communicated by your competitors. This battle is fought in customers' minds,.

Hence, it's essential to understand the context or "competitive scenario": who your competitors are and what is their Brand Positioning.

The context is composed by

- Competitors: what they do and say
- What are thinking the Customers in the Category you are competing
- What these Customers think of your Competitors
- What these Customers think of you, your company or Brand)

The Brandshot

In these years I have always recommended my clients to use the Brandshot as the tool for this competitive context analysis.

Brandshot is a method that I have developed (based on some indications that Jack Trout, the inventor of Positioning, gave in one book) as a specific market research method for Brand Positioning.

In fact I explain it thoroughly in my course MakeYourBrand as the optimal solution for the Brand Positioning Formula.

Brand Positioning Formula

The Brandshot goal is to make a "snapshot" of what is in the mind of customers about the category and the competitors.

However, I decided not to focus on the Brandshot in this course and I tell you why.

In the over five years I have taught the Brandshot method and I have used it for my clients, I have seen that, in most cases, we didn't have enough market information to use the Brandshot.

I realized that this tool, that should be ideal, it's probably suited only to markets where there are well known brands with relevant advertising investments.

But in the market where small business operate, in local markets or usually in B2B (Business-to-Business) markets, where brand awareness and advertising investments are usually much lower than in consumer markets... customers simply haven't a clear idea about competitors in their mind.

In other words: if you are a small business or work in a local market or in B2B, it's very probable your competitors aren't doing effective marketing, if any.

And so, there is a very good chance you can define your Brand Positioning as if you would operate in a virgin or unbranded market (one without any relevant brand in customers' mind).

How to define context in virgin and unbranded markets

In my experience, this is the situation small business are facing more often.

Brand Positioning Formula

What I mean is that you surely have competitors, but probably where aren't strong brands you compete with. In the customers' mind there aren't brands that clearly own a "category mountain". There will be instead "undifferentiated suppliers" and the choice will be made based on price.

How shall you work in this case?

These are the simple steps I recommend:

1) Make a direct evaluation (alone or, even better, with coworkers or employees) if, according to your experience, there are important brands in the category you compete in.

2) If, as an insider, it is hard for you to identify competitor brands, you can assume customers don't know any brand in this category. You can consider this market as "virgin" and go to step 4.

3) If, on the other hand, you can identify strong brands, keep them in mind (write them down) for the evaluation you will do in step 6.

4) In this step you shall identify the "important promises" for customers in your market. I am sure that, as a market player, you will know them. List them in order of importance. You will see there are "common promises" that every competitor have. And you will also find that some are "distinctive" and can make a difference. List the distinctive promises next to the

Brand Positioning Formula

competitors list.

5) Ignore the "common promises": they are irrelevant for marketing purposes. This mean they are typical of the category, a "playing base", something customers give for granted.

6) Focus on the "distinctive promises", the ones some competitor can have, or you can have (or not). These are the ones you shall work on to find your Differentiating Idea (see next Step 2).

7) Ask yourself if the strong competitors you have found are famous for one of the "distinctive promises". If the answer is "yes", write a connecting line between the competitor name and the promise. If the answer is "no" ask yourself why you know the competitor and write down the reason next to the competitor name.

At the end of this process what you will have got:
- You have understood if there are strong brands in your category that compete with you
- If there are, you have understood why, in your opinion, they are strong
- If there aren't, you have understood you're competing in what can be considered a "virgin market"
- You have identified promises and ideas you can use to "create a difference"

Brand Positioning Formula

If you want to make this process even more significant you can involve customers or even potential customers (ideally both) and get answers from them.

On the other hand, you have to take into account, this could lengthen the time and that often you will not get more or better information than the ones you get from a "desk research" that you have done yourself or with people from your company.

Obviously, if you have market research for your category (you can often find good information on the Internet) you can use it to integrate your considerations.

However, I speak from experience here, as an entrepreneur you should already have the "market sensitivity" about competitors and what customers want.

The real difficulty is in the next step: *find the Differentiating Idea.*

STEP 2
Find the Differentiating Idea

The very essence of an effective Brand Positioning is the Differentiating Idea.

That means, how your product or service – or, better, your brand promise – makes you different from competitors.

Finding an effective Differentiating Idea is the most important action in a Brand Positioning strategy.

The history of the Differentiating Idea

I want briefly tell you how the concept of Differentiating Idea evolved from when it has been proposed to the method I explain in this course.

It is an evolution of the concept that has taken me almost 10 years to complete.

It's important to remember first person to propose "differentiating ideas" as a possible practical Brand Positioning strategy: *again Jack Trout*.

In 2000 he wrote a revolutionary book on Brand Positioning: *Differentiate or Die*.

In this book he presented an "operating strategy" for Brand Positioning – differentiation – and a list of effective and non effective differentiating ideas.

In the book Trout presented a list of 9 effective differentiating ideas. However – from my experience in the years – they haven't the same importance and effectiveness.

In 2001, I wrote a free report called "Brand Positioning Toolkit" – downloaded by thousands of people during the years – that has been my first work to create an "operating manual" for Brand Positioning.

In that ebook I presented the differentiating ideas of Trout's book but I organized them in a more practical way.

Brand Positioning Formula

In the years, I have refined more my evaluation of Differentiating Idea.

For my online course I have identified one key Differentiating Idea that works in most situations and two specific variants that sometimes can be a better solution.

The method I explain in my course is still valid and I keep using it. However, in the Brand Positioning Formula I streamlined even more the list of Differentiating Ideas you can use.

What you find here is what I have learned in years of teaching and doing hundreds of consulting sessions.

1) "Specialist" Differentiating Idea

People like business specialize, that they focus totally to make a specific product.

The specialist is the company that does just one thing or at least works in a very narrow field, so it does that thing better than competitors that do more things.

General Electrics, the company founded by Thomas Edison that is an institution and means "electric", makes all kinds of electric devices – even power plants – but is not a leader in any electric device category.

In the Brand Positioning war, the specialist, the brand that does just one thing, always beats the generalist, the brand that does more things.

This is the simplified reasoning in customers' mind:

"If they are specialists, it means they have more experience and spend more time and resources on this thing. Hence they will make it better than another company that has to divide time and resources on multiple products".

So, when a customer chooses a specialist, this is the reasoning:

"The specialist is the best in doing this thing: so my risk is lower and my choice is smarter and I get more for my money"

Clearly this thing is not necessarily true, but it's true in the majority of cases. Surely there is a cliché at work, but we have to use clichés for our advantage.

A classic case history of the specialist advantage is *Red Bull*.

Brand Positioning Formula

CASE HISTORY: Red Bull

A clear case of the strength of a specialist is Red Bull.

Notwithstanding over 270 competitors (just in the US) with giants like Coca-Company e PepsiCo, Red Bull has 30% of the market.

That is twice the share of the second brand Monster Energy with 14% (by the way, this is another specialist brand!).

In comparison, the brands launched by Coca-Cola Company e PepsiCo have a market share about 1/15 of Red Bull's and shrinking.

Red Bull has only one product. And it's not just the energy drink specialist: it's the brand that invented the category.

(They have also a cola and a line of flavored drinks, but with irrelevant market shares and no impact on the specialist image)

You can see the mental scheme at work in the customer minds:

"I buy Red Bull because it's the specialist, so it will be the best energy drink".

In order to make this strategy to work is that the specialist brand stays like that and doesn't start to expand in other areas that the customer can consider "out of their league".

In short, the specialist brand shall not, at all cost, become victim of the "line extension" mistake.

Brand Positioning Formula

The mind doesn't want confusion: if a brand means "product category A" (e.g. fabric) it cannot mean "product category B" (e.g. sunglasses). If you think this is a weird example, I have seen recently an ad for a famous fabric brand promoting its new line of sunglasses.

This is the mistake of "line extension" (also called "brand extension") that apparently is a good idea ("let's use a strong brand to launch a new product") but in reality is a terrible idea. Why?

Because not only it doesn't create an effective positioning for the new brand, but risks to weaken the positioning of the original brand that is no more clear "what it stands for" (it happens more often than you think).

And specifically, a specialist Brand using line extension risks even more than a generic brand: when a specialist loses its specificity, it loses everything.

The "Specialist" Differentiating Idea has, however, an important limitation: you cannot use it if your market is too small.

It's not that it doesn't work in small markets, it does. But you end up having too few customers.

That is why I usually don't recommend it for small business and local markets.

In general, if your market is local and of small size, try to have the widest possible Brand Positioning.

Example:

If you create websites, you can specialize in making sites "for dentists" if you work at least at national level (state level for the US) but not if your market is your town.

Brand Positioning Formula

This is one of the subtleties of Brand Positioning: I want you to know them because I have seen too many small businesses get into a trap like this.

Summing up, the "Specialist" Differentiating Idea works because it exploits the cliché "the one who makes only one thing, has more experience and gives me less risk and more value".

And it's not difficult to put in practice. To be a specialist you don't need to do complex trick: you just have to understand how to "narrow" your product or service so you can create the perception of more experience.

However, I don't recommend to use it in a market that is too small.

Ask yourself:
What can my brand be a specialist of?

2) "N.1" Differentiating Idea

As I said, in the last few years I have used another Differentiating Idea in place of the "Specialist". A very simple and yet effective one: the N.1 or Leader.

What about?

You have to evaluate if you are N.1 in your market (typically for a specific parameter) and declare that to the market.

At first sight it doesn't even seem a real Differentiating Idea, but trust me, it's an excellent one. If you can use it... definitely use it.

Brand Positioning Formula

The goal of Brand Positioning, is to get to the point where you are considered the only viable solution for customers. The best way to achieve that is to communicate you're the N.1, the leader.

And here is the best part: most surely in your field nobody knows who is N.1. There are no specific benchmarks, no juries.

Clearly there are revenue data you can find. But there can be so many other data: # of clients, of years in the market, of products, of stores, who launched first product X, who launched new functions... and so on.

You can surely find if there are relevant parameters where you are N.1. If you can find it, then you can communicate "to be N.1", no need for specifics.

The effectiveness of the "N.1" Differentiating Idea is inversely proportional to marketing activities and brand awareness in the market.

Yes, I am saying you can own the "N.1 position" *just saying it*.

For my experience, if you can sustain your declaration of leadership for at least one relevant parameter, you can do it.

Frankly, my experience shows that in many cases, I had clients with a leadership they didn't communicate! Clearly I convinced them to use the "N.1" Differentiating Idea and it worked very well.

This Differentiating Idea and the connected Brand Positioning strategy is well told in the marketing battle between the two most important beer brands in Brazil: *Brahma and Antarctica*.

CASE HISTORY: Antarctica VS Brahma

For many years the two biggest beer brands in Brazil have been Antarctica and Brahma.

Usually, Antarctica was the slightly most famous brand and Brahma was close second.

And it was really the "undeclared" leadership of Antarctica that let Brahma use the "N.1" Differentiating Idea.

Brahma started an advertising campaign declaring it was the N.1. But at the time Antarctica was the leading beer brand.

But when the advertising campaign ended, Brahma had really become, the N.1. Customers have started preferring it to drink the "N.1 beer in Brazil".

The reality has been modified by marketing and the "N.1" Differentiating Idea.

But... what? Don't competitors say anything?

Well, while it's always better to have some relevant data to support the "N.1" declaration – but as you have seen with the above case history, they can even be absent – competitors can do very little.

Remember that marketing is a battle of perceptions and take into account the mind limitations. If you are successful in communicating you are the "N.1", your customers' mind will file that and raise barriers to other messages that try to counter it.

Clearly, if you choose the "N.1" Differentiating Idea you cannot be shy: you have to push to the metal the "we are N.1" message and communicate, communicate, communicate.

Ask yourself:

Can I be a N.1 Brand?

3) "Magic Ingredient" Differentiating Idea (extra)

The "Magic Ingredient" concept can be used in two ways:

- As a Differentiating Idea
- As a reinforcement for the other Differentiating Ideas

This concept is appreciated by students of MakeYourBrand because it stimulates creativity.

Let's see what it is all about.

People love a "Magic Ingredient":

- the red sole for Louboutin shoes
- PageRank for Google
- the blue grains in washer soap
- Steve Jobs for Apple ☺
- the yellowfin for canned tuna

If you think about it, you can find successful brands with a "Magic Ingredient" in all markets.

Brand Positioning Formula

Even the local burger place has a "secret sauce", if you notice.

In general, the more complex is your product or your category, the better a "Magic Ingredient" can work as a Differentiating Idea.

And you don't have to explain the "Magic Ingredient"... because it is, exactly, magic. But you have to communicate in an impactful and emotional way.

And the "Magic Ingredient" doesn't need to be a real ingredient. It can be a production technique, "how the product is made". If you are in services and have a specific method, you can use it as "Magic Ingredient".

Or it can be you, a personal brand if you have the clout. Like it worked for Steve Jobs and Apple.

The most fascinating thing of the "Magic Ingredient" is this: you can use even if it's not exclusive of you, if it's something that is even "standard" in your market, but no competitor used it.

The trick is to be the first to put this "Magic Ingredient" Differentiating Idea in the mind of the customer.

Let's see a "classic" case history on the "Magic Ingredient": *Schlitz beer.*

CASE HISTORY: Schlitz beer

Perfection of 50 Years

Back of each glass of Schlitz Beer there is an experience of fifty years.

In 1848, in a hut, Joseph Schlitz began brewing. Not beer like Schlitz beer of today; but it was honest. It was the best beer an American had ever brewed.

This great brewery today has new methods. A half century has taught us perfection. But our principles are 50 years old; our aims are unaltered. Schlitz beer is still brewed, without regard to expense, according to the best that we know.

We send experts to Bohemia to select for us the best hops in the world.

An owner of the business selects the barley, and buys only the best that grows.

A partner in our concern supervises every stage of the brewing.

Cleanliness is not carried to greater extremes in any kitchen than here.

Purity is made imperative. All beer is cooled in plate glass rooms, in filtered air. Then the beer is filtered. Then it is sterilized, after being bottled and sealed.

We age beer for months in refrigerating rooms before it goes out. Otherwise Schlitz beer would cause biliousness, as common beer does.

Ask for beer, and you get the beer that best suits your dealer. He may care more for his profit than your health.

Ask for Schlitz, and you get the best beer that the world ever knew.

Ask for the brewery bottling.

This is an historical case history (over 80 years old) that is a classic of the "Magic Ingredient" Differentiating Idea.

In this case the "Magic Ingredient" was a standard production method that no competitor used before.

In the US beer market of the '20s, Schlitz beer was losing market share and asked the famous copywriter Claude Hopkins to help.

Hopkins studied how the beer was made and found many fascinating production processes, each of them could have been a "Magic Ingredient".

When the Schlitz people told Hopkins those were standard methods in the beer industry, he said "So what? Competitors don't say it. You do and will own it".

So they used all those "Magic Ingredients" in advertising: "live-steam washed bottles", "plate-glass rooms where beer could cool without impurities", "4,000 foot deep artesian wells".

All these "Magic Ingredients" sustained the promise that Schlitz beer was "the purest of beers".

And so, purely thanks to Brand Positioning (well before it was defined as such) and marketing, the Schlitz beer went from 15th to market leader.

Brand Positioning Formula

As I said above, the "Magic Ingredient" can be used in two ways:

- It can be your Differentiating Idea, that is "your brand is the one with the Magic Ingredient"
- It can be a reinforcement for the two other Differentiating Ideas: "Specialist" or "N.1" "thanks to the Magic Ingredient"

Important: it's not always possible or necessary to have a "Magic Ingredient". And I remark this because, in my experience, entrepreneurs always try to find one.

It's not mandatory. But if you can find it, it can be very effective for your Brand Positioning.

Ask yourself:
Can I have a "Magic Ingredient"?

And that is everything you need to know about the Differentiating Idea and how it works. Now you have to find yours.

And when you have found your Differentiating Idea, you have to test if you have found a good one. Or not.

If the Differentiating Idea has legs.

This is what you do in Step 3: test your Differentiating Idea.

Brand Positioning Formula

STEP 3
Test the Differentiating Idea

After you found your Differentiating Idea, you need to to 2 simple tests that are however key to find the strength of your idea.

In fact, you will find Differentiating Ideas that looks good but that don't pass these tests.

If the idea doesn't pass the tests it means it would be too weak, not effective for a strong Brand Positioning.

The 2 tests you have to do are:

- Opposite Test
- Limits Test

Opposite Test

Is there anybody else who has a Brand Positioning that is the opposite of yours?

If there is no competitor with an opposite Brand Positioning you have a problem.

"Our Brand Positioning is to offer a service personalized on customer's needs" is not an effective Brand Positioning. This because there won't ever be a competitor focused on "offering a service that is not personalized and don't care about customer's needs". Do you get the concept?

An effective Brand Positioning needs that someone or even many others have make an opposite promise to the customer. Because only in this way you can differentiate yourself and create a new category where you can be the leader.

An "honest politician" is not a good Brand Positioning (no politician will tout himself as dishonest... even if he could be the most sincere). A "entrepreneurs oriented" politician is a good Brand Positioning (because there will be other politicians that are focused on employees).

In my experience the Opposite Test is very important because it solves one of the typical problems entrepreneurs find when looking for a Differentiating Idea: the problem of "saying what everybody says".

Quite often, in fact, when entrepreneurs asked me my opinion on their Differentiating Idea, I was looking at ideas that weren't differentiating at all.

Possibly interesting ideas, creative ideas, fun ideas... but ideas that were already used in their market, ideas that any competitor could use (and many were already).

For this reason, the Opposite test is the first key test for your Differentiating Idea.

Ask yourself:

Who is saying the opposite of this Differentiating Idea?

Limits Test

What limits your for your Brand?

A Brand Positioning is something really specific. A Brand cannot be several different things.

Brand Positioning Formula

It's like the classic "short blanket": either it leaves your shoulders uncovered or your feet. Or, if you prefer, like a teeter totter: when a meaning goes up, another must go down.

For this reason, you have to accept to give your Brand some limits. You have to be ready to say "Our Brand doesn't do this, we don't serve this market".

I know this is a painful concept: giving up market opportunities.

But it is a must and the reason are always the mind limitations.

I list them here:

- The mind is limited
- The mind hates confusion
- The mind hates change

If you communicate "our ALPHA product does X" and you are successful in communicating your message, the mind will create an idea that "the product ALPHA does X".

And since knowledge is difference (we learn new things by comparing them with something we already know), the mind of our potential client will do these reasoning: "product ALPHA doesn't do Y and doesn't do Z because the product BETA does Y and the product GAMMA does Z".

Or "I believe ALPHA does well X because I know it doesn't do well Y or Z".

In this way our mind learns and solves the problem of confusion.

However, if your message would be "our product ALPHA does X, Y and Z" here come the barriers of your customer mind and the whole believability of your message weakens.

Brand Positioning Formula

That is why it's important that you find what are "intrinsic" limits in your Differentiating Idea.

Remember: in every positivity there is a Ying and a Yang.

So, there surely be limits and you have to find them because they will help you to make your message credible.

Moreover, identify and communicate your Brand limits – hence a "weakness" – gives you a psychological advantage in communication.

Because, if you "share your weakness", you will have 2 advantages with your prospects:

- They will think you are honest and will be more open to believe to what you say, even when you promote yourself
- They will think you have the "complementary attribute", since you are open to admit your product is lacking in some attribute

A famous direct marketing letter that has been written for American Express starts like this:

Quite frankly, the American Express card is not for everyone.

The American Express card is more expensive and has a more complex approval process compared to all the other credit cards. Hence it is not given to anybody, because it won't be as profitable. And so American Express admits this limit that strengthen the Brand Positioning "the credit card for the rich".

Macintosh, the computer for the rest of us.

The Macintosh computer wasn't made for computer experts, because its operating system didn't allow tweaks and "getting inside the hood" and the mouse and windows interface didn't seem for "real computer users". (This happened in 1984)

For these reasons, Macintosh decided not to talk to current computer users (at the time still very geeky), who were ok with the complexity of the PC and communicated to be "the computer for those who don't get computers".

Today, after over 30 years, this Brand Positioning keep working, even if it's no more expressed literally in advertising. It is a given Macintosh computers are for people who "don't get computers" and need an user interface that's simpler than Windows computers.

Ask yourself:

What limits has this Differentiating Idea?

STEP 4
Brand Positioning Statement

Writing the Brand Positioning Statement is the final step.

The Brand Positioning Statement is a tool that you shall use internally in your business to manage your Brand Positioning.

In fact, a problem common to all businesses – even after they have defined their Brand Positioning – is how to effectively communicate the Brand Positioning.

Usually, after a while, entrepreneurs forget what they must communicate – for this they could often blame consultants and ad

Brand Positioning Formula

agencies they use – and they dilute or even nullify the effect of Brand Positioning in their business.

The 3 things you must always to keep in mind: Brand Positioning shall be communicated, communicated and communicated. Always and constantly, without any "creative" variation.

- How can you remain focused on your Brand Positioning?
- How can you know if a message is right or wrong?
- How can you teach your Brand Positioning to the whole company and new hires (or new suppliers and partners)?

The tool to do all this is the *Brand Positioning Statement*.

It is a simple tool, but, for this very reason, extremely effective.

Its duty is:

- to communicate the brand name
- to communicate what the product is / what you do and what is the market
- to communicate the Differentiating Idea

Brand Positioning Statement *(model)*

<brand name>
is <what it is & what the market is>
that <Differentiating Idea>.

Unlike competitors that
<what competitors do>
we <what we do differently>.

And this for customers means
<benefits of our offer>.

This model is incredibly simple and yet powerful and now I will explain how it works and how to use it.

What the Brand Positioning Statement is and how to use it

But what the Brand Positioning Statement is? It is a formula, a model that becomes a simple and clear explanation of your Brand Positioning.

It becomes a half-page document that you have always to have handy and that shall be known by the people who work with you.

It is the "filter" that you use to evaluate all the communication activities your business will do to communicate the Brand Positioning.

Some companies have a "company mission", but too often it is only a collection of pompous and empty sentences aiming at motivation and good intentions. Basically, it never helps to do effective marketing.

The Brand Positioning Statement, on the contrary, is a practical tool and I will show you how to use it.

But let's analyze it.

Brand Positioning Statement: analysis

<brand name> is <what it is & what the market is>

This first part seems too simplistic, but it is very important because it helps you to define exactly what your business does in one or two words, without beating around the bush.

The part "what the market is" helps you to be simple and clear and "talk like a customer" without inventing made-up markets.

that <Differentiating Idea>

In this second part you have just to write down your Differentiating Idea. Again using as few words as possible and being as simple and clear as possible.

Unlike competitors that <what competitors do>

This second paragraph starts the explanation of the difference between your business and the competitors. As usual, the words between "< >" shall be written as clearly and simply as you can.

we <what we do differently>

This part of the Brand Positioning Statement is the heart of the model. Here you explain what you do in a different way from competitors.

When we will see how to use the Brand Positioning Statement you will see how this part is key to drive all the communication you do for your Brand Positioning.

and this for customers means <benefits of our offer>

This last part adds an important element: the benefit. Since we "sell with benefits" if you clarify the benefits here, it's easier for you to communicate them.

Let's see now some examples of Brand Positioning Statements.

I just made up these examples, but by reading the Brand Positioning Statements below, you will understand well what they do, what they do differently and the benefit they give customers.

Brand Positioning Statement: examples

Example: Butter Cookie

<Butter Cookie>
is <a brand of cookies>
that <makes only butter cookies>.

Unlike competitors that
<use various, industrial fats to make their cookies>,
we <use only butter >.

And this for the customer means
<butter cookies like they are "home made">

Example: Accountant for startups

<Johnson Accounting>
is <an accountant>
who <is focused on startups>.

Brand Positioning Formula

Unlike competitors that
<serve any kind of companies>
we <serve only startups>.

And this for the customer means
<we know better how to help them solve their specific problems>

Example: Martial arts apparel

<Karate Kid>
is <a brand of sport apparel>
that <makes only martial arts apparel>.

Unlike competitors that
<offer apparel for any kind of sport>
we <offer only martial arts apparel>.

And this for the customer means
<better "specialized" performances>.

How to write your Brand Positioning Statement effectively

In my experience with hundreds of entrepreneurs I have helped to apply Brand Positioning, I have seen that defining an effective Brand Positioning Statement requires a bit of trial and error process.

The most common mistake I have seen is to complicate the model by writing a lot of text that makes it into a document that is not useful.

Here is an example I have made with a fictitious brand of this mistake (WRONG) and then an example of what a Brand Positioning Statement for this brand should be (RIGHT).

Brand Positioning Formula

I have hidden the brand name and some details, but it actually comes from a real Brand Positioning Statement a client of mine wrote and the corrected version I helped him to make.

Brand Positioning Statement (WRONG)

FAKEBRAND is a company specialized in GIZMOS, that focuses on the management of RED machines, making sure they constantly work correctly and according to standard security conditions.

Unlike competitors that do all kinds of services and consider GIZMOS as one of the several activities and don't employ specialized workers, we have been working on GIZMOS for over 30 years, have a team of specialized experts that monitor performance 24/7, 365 days at year.

And this for customers means getting very high standards of management of RED machines and of X, Y, Z parameters thanks to our specialization in GIZMOS.

As you can see (or, better, can't see) this Brand Positioning Statement is not useful to understand the Brand Positioning of this company.

And it cannot be used easily to evaluate advertising messages and ideas and see if they are correct or not.

I helped the client to simplify it like that:

Brand Positioning Statement (RIGHT)

FAKEBRAND is a company that makes GIZMOS for the management of RED machines.

Unlike competitors offering various services other than GIZMOS with non-specialized workers sharing time among different activities, we are specialized in GIZMOS.

And this for customers means we can manage their RED machines 24/7 e 365 days at year.

See how simple a Brand Positioning Statement has to be?

Basically it has to work "at a glance".

So, don't put everything inside your Brand Positioning Statement. On the contrary, *slim it down*, make it as summarized as possible, but still totally clear and easy to read and understand.

And how do we use the Brand Positioning Statement?

Let's see..

How to correctly use the Brand Positioning Statement

Let's use one of the previous examples:

Brand Positioning Formula

<Butter Cookie>
is <a brand of cookies>
that <makes only butter cookies>.

Unlike competitors that
<use various, industrial fats to make their cookies>,
we <use only butter >.

And this for the customer means
<butter cookies like they are "home made">

Now, let's see some communication examples to understand if they are *right* or *wrong* according to the Brand Positioning Statement.

HEADLINE

Butter Cookies. Cookies made like back in the days.

Wrong

It doesn't communicate the Differentiating Idea: "made like back in the days" doesn't mean "made with butter". Words have meaning.

Brand Positioning Formula

FACEBOOK POST

IMAGE
Cows in a meadow

TITLE
We are making the Butter Cookies

Right

A funny way to communicate "butter" (that in this case is also the Magic Ingredient).

PPC AD (Google Ads)

Butter Cookies – The cookies made with real butter
Ad www.buttercookies.com

We use real butter in our cookies. Just like mom used back in the days.

Right

The whole ad is on "cookies made with butter".

Brand Positioning Formula

TV commercial

Youngsters stealing cookies from each other to eat them.

SUPER
Butter Cookies.
Irresistible taste.

Wrong

The focus is not on the Differentiating Idea, but on a generic "cookies so good you can't resist" that is not differentiating from other cookies.

SPONSOR

Sponsoring a female volleyball team.

Wrong

There is no way sport can be useful to communicate the Differentiating Idea (that possibly goes in the opposite direction than sport).

Brand Positioning Formula

Do you understand how it works?

Using the Brand Positioning Statement you can, literally "at a glance", understand if the communication you want to do – or your ad agency is proposing you – is right or not for your brand.

The Brand Positioning Statement is really the "Brand Positioning juice", the final result of all the thinking work you have done so far and also the "guide" to put in practice – in the right way – the Brand Positioning you have created.

Brand Positioning Formula

Now you are Indiana Jones...

And now, you have the Brand Positioning Formula.

It can really make the difference for your business, your brand or your client's brand (if you are a consultant or agency).

Brand Positioning Formula

A final word of caution: The Brand Positioning Formula process is relatively simple, *but not that easy*.

This means *it requires thought.*

It requires that you think thoroughly at all the steps, and especially in finding the Differentiating Idea.

Take your time, try, experiment, ask for feedback.

When you will have created your Brand Positioning you will be way ahead of all your competitors.

Now you are Indiana Jones and the Brand Positioning Formula is your gun when facing competitors with a sword.

I am sorry for the poor souls of your competitors.

BONUS CHAPTER
Final words from Jack Trout

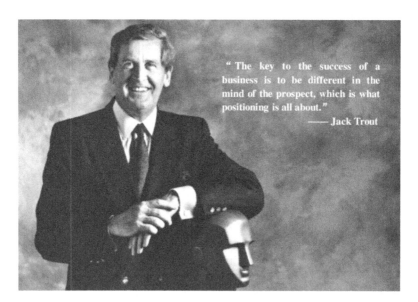

In February 2017 I had the privilege to interview Jack Trout, for my book on positioning *("Zero Concorrenti" –English version to be published soon)*.

In the interview I had the chance to ask a few questions about Positioning to the *"father of Positioning"*.

Specifically, how Positioning was invented and how it works in today's marketing environment and for small business. And Jack added some other things about storytelling and the future of Positioning.

How can it be better than that?

The Positioning concepts you find in this book... have been approved by the inventor of Positioning himself!

This is the last interview Jack Trout gave and this add even more value to this already rare event.

The marketing legend, passed away less than three months later, in June 2017.

In the following pages, you can read the interview transcript. I edited it slightly for easier reading.

Interview with Jack Trout, February 2017

Jack: Marco, how are you?

Marco: I'm really excited to call you.

Jack: Okay. All right. I got your questions.

Marco: Okay, good.

Jack: So, I would say that your first question, right, how did you come out with the positioning idea?

Brand Positioning Formula

Marco: Yeah, exactly.

Jack: It was an observation I made working with Ries. You know, this is back in the late 60's when I first wrote this article.

Marco: Yeah.

Jack: I began to see that the world was getting more competitive, very competitive. And Essentially I realized in the world of competition it's all about perception.

Marco: Uh-huh.

Jack: You win or lose in the mind of your prospect and building perceptions. So it's not a question of reality as much as perception. "Perception is reality" is the line we used. So I began to notice that it became more of a "perception game" and that was really what gave birth to "positioning yourself in the mind".

Marco: Okay, but let me ask you: at the time the USP ("Unique Selling Proposition" a concept popularized by Rosser Reeves that originated in the '40s – Editor's note) was a similar idea...

Jack: Well, yeah it started with the Unique Selling Proposition by Rosser Reeves and then the next big body of work that arrived was essentially David Ogilvy's work on the image of a brand, as opposed to the actual product difference [as in the USP]. Essentially I then went to the next level, with the "perception of a brand". Those are the three phases of how this philosophy evolved.

Marco: Yeah, because I think a USP is not considering competition. I think the "big idea" in positioning is considering competition.

Jack: That is correct. One thing that has changed in the world that people ask me all the time in the world, what has changed? I'll say I'll give it to you in one word: competition. The level of competition,

Brand Positioning Formula

that's what's dramatically changed the world of marketing, the world of politics... And now competition is on a global scale, which never existed back in the 60's.

Marco: Right, right. Now it's so fast just to build a brand message, to send a brand message to a million people like that today.

Jack: It's getting very hard, I mean with the level of competition, that's your problem.

Marco: But what are you instead of Ries? Did you have different roles in the agency, you were more the writer? How did it happen?

Jack: I was, essentially I was both. I was basically a copywriter.

Marco: I didn't know that! You were the copywriter...okay.

Jack: I was the writer and essentially I did a lot of writing and whatnot. I also handled clients because it was a small agency. So we weren't as divided up, which is see in the big agencies. You're in the account side. You're on the creative side. I was a writer.

Marco: Me too by the way.

Jack: The next question is: "Do you own the positioning concept?" Yes. I think even Ries acknowledged that I was the founder and the father of positioning.

Marco: Got it. That's it. Yeah, they decided to go more on branding and all that stuff.

Jack: That's correct. When he left on his own with his daughter he decided to go from branding, recognizing that I was really attached to positioning.

Brand Positioning Formula

Marco: Yeah, absolutely, you are the father of positioning. In my opinion you made a next level with "Differentiate or Die" *(a book of Jack Trout where he introduces the concept of 'differentiation' – Editor's note).*

Jack: That's correct.

Marco: Because in "Differentiate or Die" you told people "how to do it": the differentiation concept is amazing.

Jack: That is, that is right. Absolutely correct. That was almost the follow on-

Marco: Yeah.

Jack: It's all about perception, but at the same time, it's all about a different perception. Which is very important.

Marco: So, "brand positioning" or "positioning" you agree is the same thing. I use "brand positioning".

Jack: Yes. They're interchangeable. How the Chinese use it, it's all about "positioning strategy". They use that term.

Marco: Okay. What about positioning for small business? That's what I focus on.

Jack: It's same deal. But the problem is, small business doesn't have the money to build perceptions. Though, in essence, the small business person has to really focus on being good at one thing.

Marco: Right, yeah.

Jack: They have to become a specialist at being good at one thing. They certainly can't compete with the big people because they don't have the resources and they don't have the resources to build a big program behind their brand.

Brand Positioning Formula

Marco: Now, the internet – the threshold has lowered, so you can things that even ten years ago were impossible... but today with the Facebook ads you can do advertising starting with $100... What do you think?

Jack: I agree. It's cheap.

Marco: It's absolutely cheap. And that's why positioning now is even more important.

Jack: Yeah, that has changed things a lot and essentially, they can now go online and not have to spend a lot of money on direct mail, a lot of money on advertising and stuff like that.

Marco: I remember a small client, they wanted to do a local radio campaign, the minimum budget was $20,000. Impossible for my client.

Jack: Buying media was expensive and you're right, the internet has reduced all the costs. Now the problem is, once you go online, it's a new medium, I agree. It's a medium you don't have to pay much for, but it's even more competitive and more crowded because everybody's there.

Marco: So that's why positioning is even more important. They have to know it.

Jack: Absolutely. It's really very important. Even as a small business, you have to define, you have to position yourself very clearly versus your competition. And whether you're doing it online or however, it's the four steps, which I've talked about endlessly in positioning. Competition, what's your point of difference and how do you support that point of difference, your credentials. And finally, how do you communicate that point of difference.

Marco: Right.

Brand Positioning Formula

Jack: That doesn't change.

Marco: The fact is, the good thing is in a small business, most competition is totally unbranded, totally unfocused, totally un-positioned. So if you do positioning, even as a small company in the small business market... you're competing like using an automatic rifle against someone using a sling. I've been doing positioning for almost 30 years and now I'm focused on small business. When my clients say something using positioning, it totally changes the competition field. Customer say, "Oh, okay, I get it now. Why you are interesting. Why you are different." Even in local markets, small markets, small resources... if they use positioning they win. It is amazing.

Jack: Your biggest problem with small business is they want to become big businesses. That is your problem, believe me. Rarely are they say "I'm happy with this business, that's it. I don't want to, I don't have to get any bigger. And that is, I want to be very good at one thing and that's very good." And what happens is, they want to continue to get bigger and grow and that's the enemy. Once you start thinking like that, you're gonna essentially slide into the trap of trying to become everything for everybody or things that you really don't have the credentials to become.

Marco: Yes.

Jack: So in a way, that's your biggest problem with small companies. I tell people, "Look. Two types of people come in to my office from over the years." You got a small company with a big idea or a big company with a small idea. But what they have is resources. The one thing they do have is resources. And I say, "Guess who I want to work with?" I'll work with the big guy any time.

Marco: Okay.

Brand Positioning Formula

Jack: It's the lack of resources that small companies have. And that makes it very, very difficult. Small companies, what they do is, they come up with a good idea and what they end up doing is they go selling it to another company.

Marco: Yeah. That's a good deal.

Jack: Exactly. Who gets the resources. So that's what happens to many in the US, that's what happens to most small companies. They eventually develop it a little bit and then sell it as quickly as they can because to somebody who's got the resources to turn it into a much bigger idea.

Marco: And again, positioning is the key.

Jack: It's the key, it really is. I mean, I had a call from some reporter who's doing a piece on the world of retail and how difficult retail's becoming. You know, because in a way, if you're in the fashion side, you get knocked off in a heartbeat and your fashion goes out of style... And then the internet shows up and people stop going into their stores, they start buying stuff online.

Marco: Absolutely.

Jack: So all they have now is their brand, which they're trying to protect, but you know what? Good luck.

Marco: But for retailers, for distribution and retailers, brand positioning is trickier that for companies making products.

Jack: Yes. Retail is a tough category.

Marco: Do you think that now is even more, you get less with "brand ladders" and more like being the leader in your own market? So the strategy has changed a bit changing from 1991.

Brand Positioning Formula

Jack: Well, look. The ladder is still the ladder. If you're the leader in your particular category, it's an enormous advantage. And essentially, in other words, you kind of own that perception, if you're very good at doing one thing, you build that perception of being "one in the mind", that's always a big advantage. Now, if you're gonna be number two on that ladder, or number two in your particular category, well, now you have to deal with number one. How do you do that? That's your next problem. So in a way, the laddering thing is still a good way to look at it, but it's still building that perception and whatnot. The key to good marketing is storytelling. You've got to find a way to tell your story. And I do a lot of work with the Chinese about improving their storytelling, I mean that's a skill that a lot of people don't have. Now, the reason I can do storytelling so well with positioning, is because I've been doing it for 50 years. I mean, I was a writer.

Marco: Yes... I didn't know that, but definitely you are.

Jack: The brand story is critical. And how you tell your story is critical. That's probably the most difficult thing and I've had problems with my Spanish partner, who probably was the first one I asked in the network.

Marco: I remember, sure. What was the problem?

Jack: They're not - he's not good at storytelling. He'd never been trained in storytelling. And most of my partners are not good at storytelling.

Marco: Interesting.

Jack: Because that's never what they did.

Marco: I was a copy, so I understand what you're saying.

Brand Positioning Formula

Jack: Now let me tell you the most interesting thing in positioning. Which you probably didn't even ask.

Marco: Okay.

Jack: Where is it all going? What's happening out there in the global economy? Now essentially, the Chinese are now where - that's where most of marketing, positioning strategy is moved out East. Big, big. In other words, in essence, what they have is enormous market and now they're getting into branding. They started with manufacturing, they can make- that was their whole economy, and now they're moving to a market based economy. In a way, positioning strategy has moved East. Dramatically.

Marco: That's interesting.

Jack: That's the whole thing. In other words, they're beginning to learn and essentially, that's where the Chinese are at right now. They're trying to move into where I started writing about this whole category when the world got competitive in 1969. Ironically, this is all happening now in China. It's as if X number of years later, now it's all moved East and they're starting where I started, in a way. In the brand building. And Chinese consulting companies they don't want to look like a Chinese consulting company, because guess what? In China, you have no credentials, if you're Chinese, people are not interested. They want to look to the Western companies like myself and other people. So that's where it's all shifted. And that's because in a way, the whole market, the whole positioning strategy market is shifting East

Marco: Yeah... That's a trend I saw. I went there in 2005, in Shanghai, and I was sensing that is gonna be the next step and now you confirmed that ten years after, they are doing this. They are trying to create global brands from China.

Brand Positioning Formula

Jack: That is correct. And I pointed out the problem they face. I said, "In certain categories," I'd been out there a lot, I said, "Certain categories, would be very difficult for you to to crack because you have a lot of enormous competitors out there. You're taking on some big, large, successful competitors and you'd better have a pretty unique idea or else they'll just run right over you."

Marco: Yes. Absolutely.

Jack: But that's the change. That's the dramatic change in positioning strategy. It's all shifted East.

Marco: Okay. Good.

Jack: All right, Marco?

Marco: Thank you very much, Jack.

Jack: Yeah, good luck.

How to go further with Brand Positioning

I have been working with Brand Positioning for about 30 years and I keep discovering new angles in my consulting with clients.

So, you probably have more questions on Brand Positioning. You want to know more.

Like... What brand name? What copy? How to put it in practice? How to know if you are doing it right? Case studies? *And more.*

Don't worry. You can find this help on my site:

www.brandpositioningformula.com

Check it out now!

And you can also contact me via email writing to

mdv@brandpositioningformula.com

It's been a honor to teach you the Brand Positioning Formula. Use it in your marketing and be prepared for almost incredible results.

To your Brand Positioning!

Brand Positioning Formula

The author

Marco De Veglia has been working in marketing since 1990. He started his career as a strategic planner in advertising agencies.

After years in the agency business, he decided to become a consultant to focus on Brand Positioning: its application and teaching mostly to small and medium business entrepreneurs.

He has created an online course on Brand Positioning *(BrandFacile)* and written the first Italian book on the subject, *Zero Concorrenti*. Both the course and the book are going to be translated in English.

Marco De Veglia lives in USA and helps clients around the world with Brand Positioning strategies.

You can reach him visiting www.brandpositioningformula.com
or writing to mdv@brandpositioningformula.com

Made in the USA
Columbia, SC
08 October 2018